D1222739

BOOKS BY DARYL HINE

The Wooden Horse

The Wooden Horse

Poems by Daryl Hine

New York Atheneum *1965*

ACKNOWLEDGMENTS: Alphabet; The British Broadcasting Corporation; The Cornhill; Glamour; Hudson Review; New Poems 1962; Phoenix; Poetry 1962; The New Yorker; The New York Times; Partisan Review; Tamarack Review. NOTE: *Don Juan in Amsterdam, Tristan, An Adolescent, The Epithalamium of Anne de Joyeuse,* and *Patroclus Putting on the Armour of Achilles* first appeared in HEROICS, privately printed and illustrated by Virgil Burnett, Fontainebleau, 1960.

Library of Congress catalog card number 65-22831
Published simultaneously in Canada by McClelland and Stewart Ltd.
Composed and printed by Clarke & Way, New York
Bound by H. Wolff, New York
Designed by Harry Ford
First Edition

TO J. M. AND J. M.

Something within me cries aloud, said the wooden horse,
And of all wounds my wound is the source;
From the hollow of my heart, arms and men drop down
And run to let their comrades in and to surprise the town.
This fraud was the reward of tedious days and weeks
When stricken was Achilles' tent and the tents of all the Greeks.

CONTENTS

I   Psyche

PSYCHE

Precious little is kept in Psyche's whatnot:
Baubles, curious postcards, clues and tangles
Of string—everything you might look for in the
Bulging pockets of thoughtless schoolboys, all but
Hands. There ought to be some connection between
The things she never wants to see again and
Those we lose. Is it quite coincidental?
Childhood's toys cannot speak and suffer later.
Snaps as evidence too are unimportant.
Even that uninventive frantic farewell
That one knew nothing one said now could alter
Turns up legible. Clues belong to someone,
Someone other again involved the love knots.

Still across an unpopulated ballroom
Under musical chandeliers that require
Dusting, consciousness stumbles after lights out,
Where the watery floor lies waxed and frozen
Clumsily without skates she slips and flounders,
Comes, ridiculous, to no false conclusion,
Fidgets, hesitates on the verge of the dance
Toward solitude gaping like a cupboard
In the place of the just about to totter.
All things figure, the world and its abysses,
In a cabinet she pretends to know, which
Others thought to be empty, as if she cared.
Candelabra let fall their notes like snowflakes.

Ask her, what is a whatnot doing in a
Ballroom? Whose is the alibi for those hours
When pretending to sleep beside her husband
She—she too has her pointless secrets; sphinx-like
Psyche complicates what was clear as day this
Morning. Say that we only have three wishes.

3

One, the easiest, is recourse to silence,
Next, more difficult, is to speak precisely,
Last, implausible, are these riddling hymnals.
Each is only a way of lying and they
Do not matter a fig. So Psyche's answers,
Whether make believe, likely or true, are the
Unique oracle where love is, and why not?

ECHO

Echo that loved hid within a wood
Would to herself rehearse her weary woe:
O, she cried, and all the rest unsaid
Identical came back in sorry echo.

Echo for the fix that she was in
Invisible, distraught by mocking passion,
Passionate, ignored, as good as dumb,
Employed that O unchanged in repetition.

Shun love if you suspect that he shuns you,
Use with him no reproaches whatsoever.
Ever you knew, supposing him to know
No melody from which you might recover—

Cover your ears, dear Echo, do not hear.
Here is no supplication but your own,
Only your sighs return upon the air
Ere their music from the mouth be gone.

BLUEBEARD'S WIFE

Impatiently she tampered with the locks,
One by one she opened all the doors;
The music boxes and the cuckoo clocks
Stopped in alarm; dust settled on the floors
Like apprehensive footsteps. Then the stores
Of silence were exposed to her soft touch:
Mute diamonds and still exquisite ores.
She had not thought the squalid world had such
Treasure to proffer, nor so easy, nor so much.

She did not listen to the hinges' groans,
Complaints in metal, warnings in the wood,
But room by room progressed from precious stones
To tears, and at each secret understood,
Exclaimed, amused, "How simple!" or "How good!"
As she took up some fragile, painted jar.
Throughout the palace doors and windows stood
Whether in dread or sympathy ajar
Upon a pale horizon seeming very far.

The open doors of summer afternoons,
The scented air that passes in and out
Ferrying insects, humming with the tunes
That nature sings unheard! She could not doubt
She was unseen, no one was about,
The servants all had gone—she wondered where:
The calm within was dead as that without,
And all about her breathed the stealthy air.
She knew she was alone, that no one else was there.

Now she attained the room of artifice.
Not a thing that grew there but was made:
Venetian glass that counterfeited ice
So close it seemed to melt, and green brocade,

The wind's most subtle movements in a glade.
Nothing was modern, everything was old,
And yet it was not true that they should fade
Though time and fashion dim the emerald.
Each was at once an image and a deathless mould.

Dazzled, she shut the door, but through the next
Saw greater good than any she had seen:
A window open on the sacred text
Of natural things, whose number had not been
Created or conceived, nor did they mean
Other than what they were, splendid and strange.
One leaf is like another, and between
Them all the worlds of difference range;
The world is not destroyed and does not cease to change.

The final door resisted all her strength,
No key would fit, the bars and bolts stuck fast.
But there she pried and worried, till at length
She opened it, knowing it was the last.
They hung on hooks, their finery surpassed
Each her predecessor's, in their lives
Less fortunate than she. There hung the past,
Putrid and crowned. And thinking, 'Love survives
The grave,' she stepped inside to join the other wives.

APPERITE MIHI PORTAS JUSTITIAE

Leaves in killing frost's embrace
Falling leave no track in air,
Nor upon the branches' bare
Limbs do dead leaves leave a trace.

Words and actions leave behind
Praise or blame, some consequence
Open oftentimes to sense,
Always present in the mind.

With leaves the summer sky was filled.
Gone, they leave an empty sky
Where by winter's clouded eye
The lifted gaze is held and stilled.

Thought, the decorative art
Of intellect, mind's summer season
Distracts till the overthrow of reason
The brain and the unbroken heart.

Beeches that when foliate
Cool green branches interwove
Shew in the now naked grove
An open door, an empty gate.

From flesh and thought's deceptive tree
Let the leaves fall, let them die.
In a disclosed, denuded sky
Open those just gates to me.

RALEIGH'S LAST VOYAGE

After the departure from the guarded quay
Under sentence of return, not 'trusty and well loved,'
Though from my hands and feet the chains had been removed
My mind, my heart, my spirit were not free.
So I set out upon the sea,
The hardly serious ocean which has proved
A Circe to so many. South and west we moved
And the name of that embarkation was the Golden Vanity.

Touched by a land wind our sails of silk and cotton
Filled in the sun, fold upon hopeful fold.
Cargo hulks with nothing in the hold,
Our ships were mortgaged, more than half rotten.
Yet has disappointment long begotten
In a captive, sad, suspect and old
For a country, Eldorado, of which he has been told
A love obscured but cannot be forgotten.

But can a love so dolorous be good?
Somewhere in the doldrums fever among the men
Established the empery of boredom, fear and pain,
A reign of spleen before an age of blood,
Till waited on by sickness the commander could
Not come on deck to greet the sight of land again.
And then contrary winds and then a hurricane.
Praised be that force by which she moves the flood.

Where into the blue the brown water drops
We anchored at the Orinoco mouth
And saw on either hand a rotting growth
Of roots and broad leaves and branches and tree tops,
Tendrils twined like snakes and snakes hung down in ropes,
Bright as angels, shrill as demons both.
A fountain flowing from the gaudy south
And heaps of snow from off the mountain tops.

At San Tomé we had an embarrassing victory.
The citadel once taken proved awkward to defend
Against the besieged become besiegers. All we gained
We lost in ambush on each daily foray.
In our dreams the mine shrunk to a quarry
Like affection which becomes indifference in a friend
Or seeking hiding. There the tale should end
But I must prove the example in love's story.

For when I thought that there could be no more,
After a night of mutiny and the captain's suicide,
I learned my dear, my only son had died
In an unwatched skirmish on an unwanted shore.
Like one who sees swing to the prison door
On the whole world locking him inside
To my only listeners, cold walls, I cried,
God knows I never knew what sorrow was before.

The days grow shorter with the darkening year.
An adventurer's life is but a barren stalk.
The History of the World ends with the Prisoner's Walk
Though far and wide it seemed, and various and queer.
At the fall of the afternoon you brought me here,
To shew me the axe, the headsman and the block.
Though you torture the dumb with silence you cannot make them
    talk.
Only the dead have nothing left to fear.

PORT ROYAL DES CHAMPS

A little darker than the sky
The hill and its relief of trees;
Snow, and the bells for Compline, cease—
Like flakes of snow the souls that die,

And in the office of the dead
Performed in the mutilated choir,
Through the prick-song of desire
Sounds in a semi-quaver, dread.

The roof is gone and of the walls
Only stumps of stones remain
Protruding from the vague terrain
That formerly was Port Royal's.

A belt of iron spikes to bind
The feeble and rebellious flesh,
This death mask and disgusting fetish
More than his Thoughts express his mind!

"When my body buried here
In damp rot has begun
Penance for a life undone,
Have mercy on a pamphleteer.

"God pardon the polemicist
Whose style, art or language must
Richly show how poor the just
In what no sinner can resist.

"For the stars are far away
And one that died a million years
Ago tonight as bright appears
As one that burned out yesterday."

THE PAVILION

Lost in an ill frequented park
The house without seemed dead,
Its pillars separate and stark
And all the space between them dark,
While brightly overhead

Night above the naked trees
Her artifice had set
Where Swan and Bear and Lion freeze;
Cold touched upon but could not seize
The fountain's vanished jet,

In its elevated air,
The simple fall of pride,
Trophies delicate and bare;
And you and I were tourists there
That elsewhere lived and died.

The portico abruptly paled.
The moon's ascending look
Loss like a monument unveiled
In cornice intimately detailed,
Or like a picture book,

As on solid silver wings,
With rich and foetid breath,
There moved within the wood of things
And underbrush of happenings
The shadow of their death

That tapped upon the windowpane
And scratched against a door,
Like one locked out who knocks in vain—
They will not open up again

Nor answer anymore—

And in her suave, continual
Premeditated flight
Let a dead effulgence fall
Upon a dedicated wall,
Whelming with her light

The singular pretension of
Each constellated star.
I marvelled at the moon, above
And mistress of a world of love
To us peculiar.

THE SCREEN

The dying child reads of the lovers' flight
Behind the screen arranged about his bed.
His eyes have all the gravity of lead
And all his thoughts the clarity of a night
Whose amorous text and images affright
The innocent. Lights out, the story read,
He wonders who they were and why they fled,
Careless whether panic was their right.

On his lips, where the kiss was bred,
Breath has fastened like a parasite.
Their shut eyes from his pupils stare ahead,
They listen for the footsteps of delight.
And lost in a sensual wilderness they might
Have starved, were they not by the infant fed,
For if the unwholesome couple are his bread
And milk, he is their appetite.

Every sense, a clue however slight,
Was once with their precaution overspread.
The life they borrowed they cannot requite,
Farther than childbed they may not be led,
Nor ever known, till one or other said,
"Do not prolong it like a tedious rite.
Our steps are false and our connection light,
Trembling we trespass where we tread."

Long after on his members fall the bright
Indulgent drops in their exertions shed.
Only in his orphanage they wed,
By anonymity accustomed quite.
Pity him? Pity them instead,
Lost in his procreation, lost from sight.
The dying child reads of the lovers' flight
Behind the screen arranged about his bed.

THE DREAMER'S DIGEST

Running I reached the tower and the gate.
The shadows said, perhaps it is too late,
The sun is setting; but the tower stood
Unmoved amid the occidental flood.
The gate gaped wide; there was no gate at all,
Only an interruption in the wall,
A breach through sleep to safety. But before
I passed, a person from the postern door-
Way beckoned with a crooked, knowing finger.
I did not choose the aged harbinger
Who muttering conducted me straightway
Into a horror chamber where there lay
Machinery of torment, knives and racks
And disembowelled bodies made of wax.
A lift-shaft in the centre of the room
Rose empty, open, up into the gloom,
Wherein smiling, before the nightmare ended
As if to an appointment you descended.

I woke at once; that is, I thought I woke.
The streets were water and the buildings smoke,
The humid air was thick with liquid trills,
The muted music of pneumatic drills.
There you walked at my side, through whose disguise
I knew myself reflected in your eyes.
Something you said or did then made me laugh;
You showed me an indecent photograph
Of you and me extended on a bed,
A canopy of cupids overhead
In lifelike flight and coupled two by two,
Smooth, naked children. We are naked too
In imitation of the infant chorus;
The act is not innocuous for us.
I told you of my dream. With sudden frown

You took out pen and paper. "Write it down,"
You said. I do, and you approve the signs
That I invent, a series of straight lines
Feathered like darts or fir trees in a row,
Descriptive of my dream somehow. You know
Their secret and the dream calligraphy
As soon as written meaningless to me.

With broken dreams we find ourselves at home
In a suburban garden. Plaster gnome
And mushroom, ornamental bird bath
Furnish the rockery, line the garden path;
The leaves of an eviscerated book
Strew our front steps. Forbidding me to look
Before I count to ten you turn and go.
Cheating, I peer in through the picture window
Where stands the Victory of Samothrace,
A statue lacking hands and feet and face,
But winged, among the withered ferns. A black
Shroud envelops her, gloved hands drag her back
Into the dark front parlour of the mind,
And the same white gloved fingers pull the blind.

All this I dreamed as if awake, perplexed
As from each dream I woke into the next.
In every one as if with my permission
In front of me or by my side went one
Of either sex, or both, and any age,
Always a grand and gentle personage.
And if with conscious guilt I tried to kiss
The calm, averted cheek, "Remember this,
Remember this," you said:
"The dead are not aware that they are dead,
But what we've seen and everything we've heard
Belongs to sleep, your wishes and my word."

IN MEMORY M.D. 1872–1962

This house is empty and its guest is gone.
Never shall be mated the white and ebony pieces.
The precious thread by which the story hung
Is snapped; and while the cage of gilt releases
The bird of paradox, its pretty neck once wrung,
And now that you may verify the thesis,
You cannot tell the truth to anyone.

Still the fact beneath the window throws
Logic's rigid network on the ceiling,
And those shadow leaves
In which the watcher all too willing
A while believes:
Not will nor intellect nor transcendent feeling,
Not goodness,—why not, goodness only knows.

But nothing is missing from the empty house,
Where the furniture will be shrouded like its master
And there is nothing else you loved, to mourn.
—Which bibelots, untouched by the disaster
Reflect that they were made not born.
Flesh decays. O so do paint and plaster,
The masterwork is soon ridiculous.

Heirs presumptive waiting in the hall
Are everywhere apparent, fingering the treasure
They had not leave to touch,
And of follies they can never measure
Murmuring How much.
A pity that you cannot leave your pleasure
To whom you wish. The will engrosses all

No sooner than the testament is read,
The griefs you wished for and the consolations,
And no one cares if you were incurably sad
Under the humpty dumpty decorations,
Who wasted life and love on what you had,
Living alone without friends or relations,
But have enough of both now, being dead.

II Sense and Sensibility

SENSE AND SENSIBILITY

A stone is thrown or falls into the water.

SENSIBILITY:
Look, the ripples have reached the farthest shore
And work among the reeds that wobble there.

SENSE:
Only because you cast the first stone.
What makes you think you have so sure an aim
So to hit the water in the centre?

SENSIBILITY:
Wherever it falls, there is the pond's centre;
It makes itself the middle with its rings
That writhe from shore to shore.

SENSE:
                                        The stone sinks,
The cause of commotion, silently,
Beneath the awakened surface of the water.

SENSIBILITY:
Consider the wake of the unerring swan
As it breaks in black and frets the brackish calm
And swims upon the reflection of the moon.

SENSE:
Her feet entangled in the curling hair-
Like snares and secrets of the waves
Underneath propell her privately.

SENSIBILITY:
I fear I fail to see just what that proves.

SENSE:
Why, all the water's whims are stiff as wire
And wear as scientific diadem
The ways by which they wander everywhere.

SENSIBILITY:

And what of the reeds that guard the unmoved shore,
Green counterfeits, whispering forgeries?

SENSE:

What of us, what are we doing here?

SENSIBILITY:

Well you said you didn't want to dance.

SENSE:

I don't know how to waltz with anyone.
But you thought if I wouldn't dance perhaps I'd walk
A mile and a half at least around the lake,
While you rode, like an aristocrat,
Who could not ride unless upon my back.

SENSIBILITY:

Running and jumping, too. Don't deny it.
I've seen you—

SENSE:

      Exercising to keep fit.

SENSIBILITY:

Fit for what if not appearances,
Like the wrinkled visage of the lake
Or the swan's sedate disturbance or the track
Of the occasional moon?

SENSE:

     Fit? Fit as the stone,
The vanished source of the water's aged look,
Fit as is the white athletic swan
Whose incessant webbed feet row along
The high ponderous galleon

Whose pompous progress is everything you notice:
Fit as the moon to change and shine upon
The changed element she influences.

SENSIBILITY:
Then that's about all you're fit for,
Who are as smooth and heavy as a stone,
Vain as the ever-self-admiring swan
Who will not move except upon a mirror;
And like the lazy moon, peculiar,
Unoriginal, and not to be wished upon.

SENSE:
The labour is what the finished work eclipses,
The purpose perfected in the artifact
Is unimportant, as the act
Obliterates decision and indecision.
Feelings are known only by their effect.

The stone is thrown with greater violence.

THE APPLE OF DISCORD

The Apple of Discord
Plucked and peeled and cored,
Stripped the polished skin,
The little seeds within
Cut out, detached the leaves,
Vegetably grieves
Its loss—why should fruit,
Thus abused, be mute?

"Then am I eaten? Truly
A sin, a shame and folly
Destructive of the orchard
Wherein I was nurtured.
The city too is finished,
The people dead or banished,
And the soldiers that surrounded
The city have disbanded
Homesick and disgruntled.
The camp has been dismantled.
The ships have sailed away.
The sheep have strayed awry.
Now are become the meadows
The pasturage of shadows.

Yet, a curious thing:
It happened in the Spring
That I first was chosen,
Long ere these flowers were frozen
Stiff upon their stalks.
Troy stands and Helen walks,
Untempted innocence,
On other battlements;
Before the tree was shaken,
Before the fruit was taken,
Before favour found me . . .
Still green boughs surround me."

TROMPE L'OEIL

There is a way of seeing that is not seeing.
Far from the true dimension of our being
Who doubts but there is that we cannot see?
More than the naive employment of the eye
On decorated wall and ceiling,
The spirit's exercise consists in telling
Not right from wrong but rather true from false.
Looking at lies the eye sees something else,
In the pattern of the painted handkerchief
The painted pins that hold it up, and if
They yield, it cannot fall, it is not real.
Reality then is nearly what we feel
The outlines of, even as it dissolves.
Figures with better faces than ourselves
In a glass conduct their brigher lives
In chambers where reality survives
Only as long as it can fool or charm.
There at least we shall not come to harm;
Therein we and our desires belong,
Where lusts like bees perish as they sting.
Accidents that elsewhere fail to happen
Befall us there: doors that do not open,
Drawers that cannot ever be pulled out.
Disenchantment waits until we doubt
Upon the magic words, "It all is painted.
A queer affair but hardly what we wanted,
A box containing everything but nature,
Not one unpremeditated creature,
A landscape in the manner of our dreams,
Its meaning just, it is not what it seems."
The shadow of a fly upon the fruit
Whose suspect flesh appears substantial to it,
The deeper, broader shadow on the fly
Of the bird that it is hunted by

In the story of the still life, and
Over both the shadow of a hand
With minatory fingers seems to hover—
Will it move? or will it rest forever
On its work, a part of its creation,
The imitation of an imitation?

Round the ceiling runs a balustrade
In perspective. There the gods portrayed
As painted men and women leaning over
Laugh and kiss and talk, none whatsoever
Bored by their old immortality.
Above their heads a prospect of the sky.
The light declining on their tinted flesh
Colours with ripeness what was lately fresh
Despite the fixed meridian of the sun.
They do not seem to know their day is done,
Themselves perfected out of all ambition,
But lolling in the attitudes of passion
Sumptuously clothed or gloriously nude,
Endymion asleep, Andromeda pursued,
Ageless nymphs and coarse priapic satyrs,
They shew the features that illusion flatters
And throw from the false Olympus of the ceiling
The long, deceptive shadows cast by feeling.

There is a way of seeing that is not sight
Like a candle lit in broad daylight
And darkness too that is not always night.

THE LAKE

dans le simple appareil
D'une beauté qu'on vient d'arracher au sommeil.

Smoothed by sleep and ruffled by your dreams
The surface of the little lake
Fed by unconscious tributary streams,
Unbroken by the breezes nightmares make,
Like your face looks fathomless and seems
Bottomless till light or noises wake.
You move and murmur and almost awake.

I admire but do not wish to enter,
Like any wanderer beside
Moonlit water in midwinter
Who as a simulacrum for the tide
Casting a pebble into the calm centre
Watches the circles spread from side to side.
I wait for you and morning at your side.

Such sources feed the mirror of your mind,
I dare not touch the surface of your sleep.
But to love by ignorance resigned,
Infatuated guardian, I keep
Watch beside a fountain where I find
No image, for images too deep,
Above your breathing regular and deep.

THE WASP

It was a wasp or an imprudent bee
Against my skin, underneath my shirt,
That stung as I was trying to set it free.
Art is perhaps too long, or life too short.

Ignorant of entomology
I watched it at the crumbs of my dessert,
Numbered its stripes, curious what sort
Of wasp it was, or what tribe of bee,

While bored, aware that it was watched, maybe,
Buzzing, it appeared to pay me court,
And darted in where I could not see
It, against my skin, underneath my shirt,

There in the sweaty twilight next to me
Its amorous antennae to disport,
But always armed. The minute, golden flirt
Stung as I was trying to set it free.

So it escaped, but died eventually,
An event exceeding its desert,
While I, stung as I deserved to be—
But art is perhaps too long, or life too short.

Trivial, scarce worthy of report,
Wonderful the wounds of love should be
Occasion, none the less, for poetry.
Thus deaths, that is the deaths of others, hurt.
                             It was a wasp.

THE LETTER

Between its narrow margins flowed a familiar stream,
Reproaches and endearments automatic as a dream:
Not pleasures nor new places, but pity was your theme.

What am I to answer? Pity is skin deep,
Pity has no private parts, pity will not keep,
Pity but affects to care for those who make her weep.

But pity was your watchword, you thought nothing of
Striking out below and scratching out above
Darling, Yours sincerely, Faithfully, and Love.

And you on the other side, and I lament on this,
Difference and distance inserted in the kiss,
Coldness, Dear, and darkness, and metamorphosis.

PLAIN FARE

(Night Thoughts on Crossing the Continent by Bus)

How slow they are awakening, these trees,
    This earth, how late they sleep
Naked. Past the window of the bus
Where wide and nameless rivers interrupt
The plain that divided us, they stretch
Like determined sluggards muttering, "Not Yet."

America, the work of a magic realist,
    Make of it what you will:
The vast and apparently pointless construction
By whom—when—for what purpose begun?
The little figures beside it to give an idea of scale;
And behind, before, about like a canvas the plain.
It is disquieting to think of anyone living here,
    And the lights one sees
Rare in the darkness to unbelievable lives belong.
We too flash on their incredulity and are gone,
Cowboy and farmer buried alive in their nest,
And me sitting up all night reading *Villette*.

Sometime before dawn another stop, for breakfast—
    Country ham
And eggs—where the unfledged travellers
Wait, their faces turned from one another
In a fine balance between friend and enemy, equally nameless,
For coffee, with weary contempt and despair.

The waitress is slow, friendly but inefficient,
    The boy is impressed,
He only knows why, with these sorry unworldly exiles.
Both smile, harried and shy. It is time,
There are miles to go before morning, but no hurry.
We have ceased to believe in arrival. I ask for tea
And must decide between milk and lemon. "Voyage"

I used to think had
To derive from the French verb *voir* "to see,"
But blind as the best I stumble back to my seat
On the bus, take up *Villette*, switch on the overhead
Light and light yet one more cigarette.

—To be puzzled and a trifle disappointed.
      The eponymous heroine
Turns out to be a place called "little city"
—Why not just Brussels, which obviously it is?
This is the saddest book, I think, I ever read. On
The cover it says that Charlotte Bronte,
After the death of Emily, Anne and Branwell
And before her marriage and death a year after,
"Wrote this history of lost love."
      And when I look up
Mine is the only light still burning in the bus
Where my faceless fellow travellers and, outside, the country
   slumber.

. . . It is day, and the lights and roadside structures have vanished.
The novel is finished and the reasons no longer exist
      For my visit. From heaven
Out of sight an audible jet
Covers in a mere hour or so
The way that I could not afford to go.

AN ENGLISH ELEGY

Light are the spinning favours, intangible tonight
    Tossed along the sheeted shores shipshape and lost
Of privacy asleep, as curious above
    Their heaps at pulsebeat intervals there creeps
South across the ceiling the eye at the harbour mouth
    In a path for waves to collapse and die in.
All-seeing, its attentions like a survey fall
Else far out to sea or through the windows of ocean-front hotels.

On shadowy counterpanes, their borrowed colours gone,
    Drunk by the darkness, on busy bodies sunk
Slothwards, on the lewd and the unlovely equally, on both
    Sexes a gleam that dazzles and perplexes,
Wakes the dreamer barely in time to his mistakes,
    Caresses the tear-spotted pillow and addresses
These, ineligible, unsuitable with a suitor's Please
Accept for you cannot refuse my advances. Believe my promises.
    All are kept.

Prim in seaside bedrooms spirit lamp, vapour and megrim
    Reign. To the prose rhythm of the rain
From disestablished skies the revelations come:
    Wrath and retribution over Bath.
Let other pens dwell on guilt and misery, who can forget
    How pride bent double in a bow,
And even prejudice made an effort to understand
Us, waking or sleeping, our ebb and flow synonymous.

Just as the pharos while harbour and ocean endure must
    Revolve round the bay and in its beams dissolve
Plaster pediment, terrace and crescent and stucco pilaster,
    While human nature persists the spinster's smile
Sees through every flirtation and the lesser hypocrisies
    With the accuracy of a report and the force of a myth.

Does she care one way or the other about the insects whose civil
    buzz
In her ear composes a hymn to good sense and the unspectacular
    nature of sin?

What does the lighthouse have to say to the waves which are not
        Either profound or constant but vary with the weather,
Outside the breakwater, beyond the harbour, never without
        Amusement or society, however dumb
Or shrill? Does the beacon consider their being a bore?
        No, for the light thinks it a duty to shew
Any form that its look may invent, and its progeny are many,
More than the difference and picturesque division between ocean
    and shore.

But the objective case of the light is open and shut,
        Accusing or perhaps merely noticing who sing
Ill, who need practise, who listen, who will
        Inherit the inadequate income of the spirit
After the loud disgrace and downfall of the kingdom of laughter.
        To certain friends and relations sensible and few
Might one from time to time confess always being right
Dear, inasmuch as not only the wise and the well-bred have ten
    thousand a year.

THE OUIJA BOARD

The wood that they prefer to walk is no-
Where. Voices blind or deaf or hungry
Swarm like bees when questioned: eager, angry,
Back and forth they make the teacup go.

"What is your name?" "Eo." "Will you let
Us use you?" "Never." "As a guide?"
"There are handbooks to The Other Side."
"Tell us the way to heaven." "I forget,

"But each new spark feeds an unvarying flame,
For each is the occasion—" "To remember?"
"The only picture in its solid frame,
Hand and cheek and thigh and lip and member."

Yet those very groves are vocal with
Unlettered mouths that kissed reply Don't Care.
Invert a glass and they breathe underneath,
Turn back to the glass and they return your stare,

And if you try to tell them of your need,
They giggle and spell nonsense, to all such
Statements as We Love You answering How Much.
Is the grave but a glade, falling leaves, and seed

For the unborn to enter and become,
A blind procession, chain of beings, loves?
Hold the planchette down between finger and thumb
On table as flat as the world is, yet it moves.

III   Tool and Die

LAST WORDS

I

The telephone keeps talking to itself:
Garbage in the streets, a butterfly,
A rubber raft abandoned, floating out to sea,
And late last night nearby, a conflagration—
If you knew half the secrets I can tell,
The accidents, the threats, the promises,
All anonymous, and the voices
That, like a demoniac, I have:
An unwilling rhyme, a cry for help,
An order for a pound of stewing beef
And someone begging someone to come back—
All of these proceed from my black mouth,
All and more are locked in my black heart,
Information, long distances, wrong numbers.

II

The clock at first was fast and now has stopped
That holds all of our lifetimes in its hands.

III

"We sleep and wake watched over by machines. Are these
intelligent objects our servants merely? Are they
our *closet* masters, maybe? Will we be accomplices and
equals one day?"

Tool-and-Die Makers' Manual
Newly revised, 1964

37

IV

The gun, the peppermill, the gramophone,
The bee, the salamander and the swan—
To be explicit, what have they in common?

The corkscrew, the stethoscope, the laundromat,
The lyre bird, the python and the wombat,
How do these differ from the domestic cat?
Is it a question of theirs and ours or this and that?

What reconciles the wireless and the whale?
Did he who made the lamb invent the wheel?
And what was wisdom doing all the while?
A catastrophe and a category will
Swallow sardines and supermarkets whole.

V

But you or rather thou, to be archaic,
Always demanding, never dull but sometimes sick,
Intimate machinery, my body!
Whose only raison d'etre is to be:
Your pleasures and your pains are your own business;
Don't ask me for a taste or a caress,
Who, when I weep, weep tear of glass,
Round and brittle. Your appetites embarrass
Me. Mine tire you. Old Thing,
The moral is, the moral is, Keep going,
And perhaps we shall meet again at the Resurrection—
The wonder is, what then I shall put on?

PATROCLUS PUTTING ON THE ARMOUR OF ACHILLES

How clumsy he is putting on the armour of another,
His friend's, perhaps remembering how they used to arm each other
Fitting the metal tunics to one another's breast
And setting on each other's head the helmet's bristling crest.
Now for himself illicitly he foolishly performs
Secret ceremonial with that other's arms,
Borrowed, I say stolen, for they are not his own,
On the afternoon of battle, late, trembling, and alone.

Night terminal to fighting falls on the playing field
As to his arm he fastens the giant daedal shield.
A while the game continues, a little while the host
Lost on the obscure litoral, scattered and almost
Invisible pursue the endless war with words
Jarring in the darkening air impassable to swords.

But when he steps forth from the tent where Achilles broods
Patroclus finds no foe at hand, surrounded by no gods,
Only the chill of evening strikes him to the bone
Like an arrow piercing where the armour fails to join,
And weakens his knees under the highly polished greaves.
Evening gentle elsewhere is loud on the shore, it grieves
It would seem for the deaths of heroes, their disobedient graves.

DON JUAN IN AMSTERDAM

"e tu allor li prega
Per quell' amor che i mena, e quei verranno."

INFERNO V

This also is a place that love is known in,
This hollow land beneath a lifeless sea
Opposite to the place that he was born in,
How far it is impossible to say.
  The brackish water as I crossed
  A bridge was delicately creased
And stained and stale, like love-disordered linen.

Lovers here must meet on unsure ground
Like strangers in a circumspect hotel
Which, although luxurious and grand,
Trembles beneath their feet like earth in hell.
  Lifted on concentric gales
  Scraps of paper, leaves and gulls
Fluttered dismally aloft and groaned.

Here darkness grows and light itself decays;
Rain falls from time to time and night falls too
Upon earth's civil centre that decoys
The eternal with the promise that is now.
  There were no corners, every street
  Ran on infinite and straight,
There is no gate, no warning and no keys.

I hear a step approaching and refuse
To look aside, a while your silhouette
Persists, the fire illuminates your face
From under as you light a cigarette;
  All-knowing, arch-angelic eyes,
  Human features cut in ice—
The spark you struck at once attained the fuse.

I recognize the vanity and scorn,
The fear, the greed, in short the mask of love,
Familiar and disdainful, and I turn
About. Like children sharing what they have
    We learned in that experiment
    What the spirit's weakness meant,
The nature of the torment to be borne.

What shall I give you? What will be your price?
Your body's mine, the rich, fantastic horde
Of your embracements—angels live on praise,
Take it, it is all I can afford.
    Outside a centrifugal wind
    Sustained a freight of souls that whined
And wept along the terrible canals.

And when I close my eyes I see a ship
At anchor in the water of a bay.
I cling to that imaginary shape
Capable of taking me away
    To I do not know what ports.
    Perhaps tomorrow it departs,
Anonymous, invulnerable, free.

TRISTAN

Again the ocean rubs against the shore
And then draws back, dragging sand and stones.
Each falling wave removes a little more
Shallow flesh from the earth's enormous bones,
And white as salt, for waves of salt consist,
Gathers in with gurgles, signs and groans
What shock of meeting has not turned to mist
Nor wrench of parting left upon the sand.
Drawn by a mass that they cannot resist,
Driven by a force which they do not withstand,
Under the compulsion of the moon,
The tides exhaust their impulse on the strand
And as they ebb grind out the sort of tune
That leaves might make that whispered in a wood
Even at the breathless hour of noon
Despite the calm in which the forest stood.
A lifeless sphere, mutable and strange,
The moon compels the ocean where she would
And makes the soft, complaining billows range
Forth and back like wind-distracted grass
Or beasts transformed or in the act of change.
Upon the sand as on a pane of glass
A summer storm inscribes its track, their flight
In shells and seaweed waves describe and pass
Back into their oceanic night,
Retreating only to renew the trial
Whose issue stretches equal out of sight.
As a shadow moves across a dial,
As the sun that moves the shadow moves,
Which passion may assert without denial,
The sea resolves her love in certain grooves—
For they are thus connected, lands and seas,
And this their fond, incessant fumbling proves—
While in her heart fish glide, anemones

42

On a sea floor patterned like a hand
Graze like sheep and sometimes sting like bees,
Like fluid bees, and crabs run sideways and
Lung-fish gasp like lovers undersea.
The waves that make their way toward the land
And hurry on the sooner not to be
Touch the arid shore and perish there.
Waves are forms the air gives to the sea,
Clouds are shapes that water takes in air,
Aerial breakers floating soundless by
Above our heads or caught beneath us where
Their slopes, their shifting sides reflect the sky
Like winds reflected in a weather vane.

O we shall die, O we shall surely die,
Every movement makes our death more plain
And waves will break in climax on the shore
And rise and fall and fall and rise again.

THE EPITHALAMIUM OF ANNE DE JOYEUSE, ADMIRAL OF FRANCE

[RONSARD: ELEGY I]

Joyous be your name, intending that in joy
A joyous life is yours forever to enjoy
Now your destiny has proudly overcome
Vexatious chance and brought your ship safe home
To harbour crowned with flowers, the hymeneal brand
Fastened to the topmost mast and lit by Eros' hand.
Cunningly the fates, the hour that you were born,
Spun out your thread of life perfect and unshorn
By premature misfortune, fatefully intending
That happiness, your happiness should never have an ending.
Scarcely had manhood's first uncertain growth
Covered your cheek, in the years of your youth,
But firm in a virtue not commonplace nor light
I saw you trample underfoot envy and despite.
Beloved of your followers, most dear to your lord,
By Mars and the Muses impartially adored,
The Muses all have praised you, and Mars whilst you were young
For honour's sake made you as valorous as strong.

In the tournament I dream I see you now,
Clad all in bright armour, a star set on your brow,
Esquired by love and carrying love's token
Amid the flying splinters of the lances you have broken,
With the steel of your strong sword afrighting those around
And striking helms and waving plumage to the ground.
Now at the barrier like lightning you appear
Casting up a wake of dust in your swift career,
Riding at the ring and bearing off the prize
From the expertest knights chivalry supplies,
In all things excellent, the hero of the hour.
Then when evening falls, at the twilight hour
When the sky is stained by the death of the day,

I picture you arming for a gentler essay,
No less skilled at the handiwork of the Queen of Beauty
Than valiant in the field when elsewhere lies your duty.
Evening, dear to lovers, draws on; I see the couch
Ringed by the dancing graces, at their touch
Decked and perfumed, the fairest of fair bowers,
Thick with lilies, roses, and many sweet-scented flowers.
Venus, to bless this night so long longed for,
In her chariot that twin swans draw
Approaches through the air and lays upon the covers
Of the nuptial couch her girdle, propitious to lovers,
Who wed by Venus' belt, emblem of all union,
Cling, and out of two are made eternal one.
And round about the Loves, fluttering their wings
Fan to flame two hearts already smouldering:
One I see, it seems, loosen your robe, which shed,
He takes you by the hand and leads you to the bed
Perfumed with suave odours; another conducts the bride,
Her bridal gown unfastened, close to the bedside,
Lending her a million graces in your eyes, so that
Such a conjunction shall never come to naught,
But flourish implicate, like the vine that embraces
The stout elm tree in true love's traces.
The Word that you have given, the Sport that you enjoy
With the dovelike kisses time must not destroy.
Let each part perform delightful exercise
In the service of love as love may advise.
And in your contentment wisely revelling
Gather breast to breast the flowers of your spring,
For the best years of youth and loving speed
And to them but death and old age succeed.
I see as in a vision the guardian of mankind
Wings upon his heels, a torch in his hand,
Hymen, high governor of family and race,

Range about the bed, each in proper place,
Singing youths and maidens, and with his holy light
Illuminate the bed and you and all the wedding night.
I hear the patterned footsteps of the dancing throng,
The whole house echo to their marriage song,
And the consort drowning with its tuneful noise
The virgin's lament that will soon make her rejoice.
Concord for evermore has raised her temple here,
Here Faith resides. O may the returning year
Bring with it a son, the image of you two,
Joyous, to make his father and his mother joyous too,
So your virtue shall, that is a Prince's pride,
And your high blood, to Lorraine allied,
Shine, a new sun, abashing with its light
Those in whom felicity inspires fear and spite.

AN ADOLESCENT

Dans le trouble où je suis je ne puis rien pour moi.

Sometimes in front of the deceptive landscape
Someone strolls and pauses, a boy no longer,
Do I recognize the unhandsome stranger
    Once he has spoken?

He who just last year led the schools of children
On the brave new heights and along the river
With the fragile voice that is now forever
    Altered and broken.

On the surface much as he was before the
Dream that brought so many defilements waking
And at which his world became queer and shocking,
    In nothing changed much

Save the way he lives and the dread he lives in
Of the heart that knows and the secret words that
Fearful he must listen to, yes, and look at,
    Sickening must touch,

Flocking thick winged instruments that at bedtime
Force him to behold the vagina's pink shell
Falsely close and falsely reopen, as well
    As the mock penis—

Surely this is not what he prays to nightly?
No more ought he trust his daylight companions,
Uncouth, dull, coarse, idle, delinquent these ones,
    Cupid and Venus.

How he wears his youth's unbecoming belted
Jacket, round his shoulders the armour of age,
Squeezing in his palm a small pen-knife whose edge
    He fingers often.

Now his eyes are full of a tasteless hunger
And his features heavy with resignation;
Set on lip, cheek, brow is the abstract passion
    Love cannot soften,

Staring out from windows where death is pregnant
Under damp curls strung on a rotting forehead
Breathing through his mouth like the fish, cold blooded,
    That in the flood stand

As he floats himself over grief and knowledge;
After childhood's wrongs have been known, forgiven,
Undiscovered still are the ways to live in
    Puberty's wasteland.

Window speaks to window as shade to shadow
Thus, 'Our blinds are drawn and our summer selves dead,
Elsewhere windows twinkle their lights abroad
    Long after sundown.

'Is it all too true what we wished for fondly,
This the very thing that we thought we wanted?
There is no way out, what we prayed is granted,
    Suddenly full grown.

'Shelter have we none, hence our broken shutters,
Tempests blow like kisses through empty spaces,
Weeping North West winds to their salt embraces
    Beg us to open,

48

'So the days are equal that soon will shorten
To the equal nights and the nights grow longer,
Venus' waiting room and the willing stranger—
      What should we hope then?'

'Open wide your arms wherein darkness lightens,
O your eyes alone may dispel those shadows,
There is no respite from the talking shadows
      Save in your silence.'

Somewhere winter falls, be it Spring or Autumn,
Through the long, cold stop, through the frozen meanwhile
There is no escape for the young but exile
      Cunning and silence.

TWIN ALLEGORIES OF SLEEP

I

To one who lay with lids agape
    And pleasure locked inside,
The wind like a procurer tried
    To show the gentler shape
The bridegroom sleep imposes on the bride.

"Beneath the heavy emblems of
    His languorous estate
He spreads with fingers opiate
    The poppy bed of love
Where you must undergo his tender weight,

Light as the feathers that oppress
    The wing-permissive air,
Dark as the secret, curling hair
    That sprouts from the wilderness
Of the pale body here and there.

Now as the April sky obscure
    When first Orion's seen,
A black and glittering machine,
    The overwhelming moor
Extends like a solid cloud, between

His inky thighs containing yours,
    His soporific dart
Drives in unconscious to the heart.
    Thus are sleepers whores
That sigh with patient breath and lips apart

Sleep's name, one syllable, a hiss.
　　Their snowy members thaw,
They say with every breath they draw
　　Obstructed by a kiss,
Enwrapped and crushed and penetrated, 'Ah!' "

The trembling pander holds his tongue,
　　At last the listener dozes.
One thinks one knows what one supposes.
　　The lullaby is sung
Too late, too long. Day breaks among the roses.

II

Le sommeil est une image de la mort.
　　And those who sleep will die
Excluded in the closing of an eye
　　By a curtained door.
For all who sleep sleep is death's metaphor.

For those who breathe their last by death surprised
　　In the middle of a dream,
For those who in their breathless pallor seem
　　More than hypnotized,
For lovers and for children unbaptized,

Morning stalks in vain the summer fields.
　　In fields of asphodel
Where summer cannot penetrate, in hell
　　Where Prosperpina wields
The power of life in exile, morning yields

To evening and evening to delight.
    To sleep is to begin
To die, to rest, and those who rest in sin
    Evening will requite
With one eternal dormitory night.

Touch them, they will not stir, nor, called to, wake
    From their oblivion.
Darkness fades and blushes before dawn
    Unseen, day does not break
Upon their souls nor sunrise for their sake.

Holy night, you fall upon the eyes
    Like dreams of meaning free!
You I love, you are sleep's effigy,
    You are death's prize.
So sleep, that you may sleep in paradise.

ANIMULA VAGULA BLANDULA

With breaking voice, late adolescent wit,
Ashamed of the exercise and the undress,
Nude, candid see the cities of the Pit
And famous views that end in nothingness,

Death's houses as peculiar as people,
Hell's vacant lots, the low and heavy sky:
Suffer the attentions of some damned disciple
Unpunished there, while heros pass you by.

Soul-kin, malkin, bawdkin, guest and friend,
Now you leave for places far unguessed
At, dark, and like a tear descend
Down cheeks all down to sympathy and rest.

IN THE MUSEUM OF SCIENCE AND INDUSTRY

Drawn by a full scale model of the heart
And the promise of a free admission,
Habitually affected to indolence, ignorance and art,
We enter tentatively the error whence any truth may start,
Unenlightened victims of the superstition
That everything must end, as it began, in a partition—
Who have but come together and do not wish to part
Just yet, content, as science never is, with our condition,
And looking forward to tonight and every new position.

Yet here is the famous pendulum that shows
—Remotest oscillation on a string—
That the world beneath us really goes
Round as they say, though why round no one knows
Except ourselves, who now know everything.
Through a heaven of inventions swing,
Or swings, above us the rows or mystic rose
Of superannuated stars; they sing
In electronic prose their ancient wandering.

Next to descend together the backward mine
Step by step against a dark decor
Where lumps of carbon shine
Like lamps, black diamonds, embalmed ancestors of the vine;
Yes, step by step and hand in hand, looking for
Un peu profond ruisseau, colomnié la mort,
We grope our way. Up? or down? No sign
Which. We hope (and fear) as tourists to explore
The shallow core of earth, death's superficial shore . . .

A knowledge of the future and the past,
What once we were and one day may become
Is not enough, collected, labelled, classed,
From the affectionate particle to this vast

Mastodon of boredom, to overcome
The staggering subtraction and momentary sum
Of things, that die before our eyes or last,
Outlast the imagined long millenium,
Eloquent things, oppressed, triumphant, dumb.

Prince of the air, what progress? Sometime, never,
When embraces shall be out of date, disdain
Mine as a too elementary lever.
Let the poor, industrious and clever
Invent an anaesthetic; you enrich the pain.
For love is a busy body; can his business explain
Each gain as loss? Or will you ever
As you travel on a higher, faster plain
Forget your first emotion in a far from model train?

THE WAVE

Suddenly it was quiet as a Sunday,
That extra day when nothing is permitted,
The first or last, whichever you prefer;
Nothing now rolled out her long drawn sway.
The bay was like a vacant nautilus
That held in vain a secret of the sea.
Even dumb things were listening: the trees,
Sentinels of the shore, had ceased their signals,
The insects grew self-conscious and fell silent.
　　Echo was dead. Dead,

Yet I think we all had the impression
That something would come to us on the water,
Music or a message or a god.
Yes, and this held all of our attention,
What was to come, whom, we must wait and see.
The afternoon was literally breathless,
Wide awake . . . Soon the promiscuous tide
As if plucked by conscience left the beach,
With a sigh the ocean fled away
　　From many a strange bed.

And to be sure it was something shocking
To see the submarine groves' unguessed-at grottos
Naked, and the shame of the sea creatures
Exposed amid the wrack of rock and weed.
At the same time, as at a theatre
To warn of the beginning of a play,
There were three knocks, not loud or close together,
Distinct and distant, like that and that and that,
A reiterated hint to imitate
　　The water's get-away:

As if across the empty sea came pirates
Guided by the inner vision of their kind
From the vague extremities that lie
Frozen half the time and furious,
Marked on no map or marked to be forgotten,
Realms of what use to the imagination?
Conventional antipodies of the exotic,
Without a name almost—without fuss or motive,
Without a wind through unimpeding calm
     Into the white bay.

I wanted to write it down in my diary
Then and there, this unexceptional moment,
Unique because like every other moment,
It yet had taught me what a moment was.
But even as I wished for pen and paper—
The smooth manilla sand, the ink dark sea—
What could I say of an event where nothing happened
Save . . .? I turned to my obstinate companions,
Waiting it seemed for wave, shipwreck or ransom,
     They stood on the shore mum

Like a person standing before a door,
Listenening maybe, that they fear to open,
Which will open of its own accord presently inward,
Aware of the vanity of every act.
One watched—the track of the sea, was it coming nearer?
Her back to us another, simpler, stared,
The faraway half focused in her eye.
Some swore or prayed—I could see their lips moving.
Someone moved his hands in isolate absolution
     Or traced a Te Deum.

What happened next do I want to remember?
Perhaps we ran, perhaps we stood our ground
And the ground removed till safe and sound we arrived,
Ashamed to count ourselves, for some were missing.
Nor could we after witnesses agree
Just how the others met their martyrdom.
The seismographic report said a sea tremor,
The serious minded saw an act of God,
Both inferring further catastrophe
    Certain and sorry.

Whether those horses rode upon the wave
As some pretend, or whether the earth yawned,
As well she might in immemorial boredom,
The mess tomorrow saw upon the strand,
The common stock in trade of dogs and gulls,
The picnic drowned, dead bodies, dying fish,
Rubbish and sea things never seen before—
So the memorabilia of the flood,
God's interrupted wish-fulfillment, told
    Some of the story.

DARYL HINE

Daryl Hine was born in 1936 in Burnaby, British
Columbia. He read Classics and Philosophy at McGill
University in Montreal, and he holds an M.A. in
Comparative Literature from the University of
Chicago. From 1958 to 1962 he traveled and lived in
France, England, Scotland, Italy and Poland. In
addition to his three earlier collections of verse, he has
published a novel (*The Prince of Darkness and Co.*, 1961),
a travel book (*Polish Subtitles,* 1962), and a brief
monograph on Sir Lawrence Alma-Tadema.

DATE DUE			